10 Practices of Highly Successful College Students

Longman

New York   San Francisco   Boston
London   Toronto   Sydney   Tokyo   Singapore   Madrid
Mexico City   Munich   Paris   Cape Town   Hong Kong   Montreal

Developmental Editor: Diana Murphy

Internet: www.ablongman.com

ISBN 0-205-30769-8

Printed in the United States of America

20 19 18   06 07 08

TABLE OF CONTENTS

Introduction

Wouldn't it be nice if we only needed to know ten things to have a happy life, or make a lot of money, or have lifelong health? Everyone knows that life's issues are too complex to be conquered with a quick and easy solution. You will, however, find that there are strategies that will increase your chances of making these things happen. Developing relationships with people you care about will help insure happiness. Applying yourself to your job will make you more successful. Eating healthy food and getting regular exercise will improve your health. You can similarly increase your chances for success in college.

College will place demands on your time and energy that significantly differ from those you experienced in high school. Add to these the pressure of going to school while working or caring for a family, and the task may seem unmanageable.

10 Habits of Highly Successful College Students focuses on the areas that are essential to college success. It is, however, only a starting point. The material is adapted from a variety of books, all of which are excellent resources for further information, and are listed on the back cover of this book. If you find a subject that is particularly relevant to your needs, consult the books listed at the end of the chapter for more in-depth coverage.

1

Managing Your Time

"Nothing is a waste of time if you use the experience wisely. " **—Rodin**

Probably the single most important thing you can do to impact your college success is manage your time effectively. Remember that you are not learning to manage your time just so you can accomplish more work. The real reward of time and priority management is that it also allows you to have more fun. So if you approach the concept of time management with the idea that you will be gaining more time to relax, go to the movies, exercise, or just do nothing, you are much more likely to stick to your plan. Developing and perfecting time management skills are critical to your success as a college student.

Using Time Effectively

From the standpoint of academic success, you should assess how well you are using your time to achieve your academic goals. Ask yourself whether you spend too much time diverting energies from tasks such as preparing assignments, reviewing notes, and studying for tests. To begin making more productive use of your time, you need to know not only how you have been spending it, but also how you want to use your time more effectively. Your attitude is critical. As with going on a diet or saving money, you have to want to improve the ways you use your time.

Changing Your Attitude Toward Time

Remember that everything begins with your desire to use your time productively and in line with your priorities. If you spend too much time watching television, for example, you need to decide just how much you will cut down. Make a list of your viewing priorities. Ask yourself some questions. Must you watch late night movies or sit-coms every night? Football games on Sunday afternoons? Rank the kinds of viewing you care most about, and cut back on the less important kinds. Also ask yourself why you might be watching too much television. Are you bored or restless? Are you watching to escape from your responsibilities? To be with friends?

Along with watching television and other leisure activities, you may also have to work or juggle other family responsibilities. In such circumstances, you may experience difficulty in making time for both the things you have to do and things you most enjoy doing. To help you get through such difficulties, try to remember why you came to college. Remind yourself of your goals and what is required to achieve them. Realize, too, that periods in your life when your free time seems minimal (or perhaps even nonexistent) will eventually end. Look forward to an upcoming vacation when your parents can help with the children, when you have a few days off work, or when you get some relief from the most intense of your time pressures.

Developing Strategies to Use Your Time Productively

You can employ a number of strategies to conserve time and use it efficiently. These include setting limits on how much time you allocate for different activities, avoiding situations that tempt you to waste time, and filling dead time, such as the time you spend waiting in lines, sitting in offices, idling between classes, or waiting for friends or family.

On days when you run errands, for example, you can carry a book or index cards with notes to study while you wait in the supermarket, in the lunch line, at the cleaners, in the dentist's office, and so on. On days when you have classes, you can use the time waiting between classes to review your notes, skim passages you previously marked in your text, or think of some questions you'd like to ask in class. Longer stretches of time between classes can be spent in the library or computer lab.

You can also use the times when you are otherwise occupied to better advantage. For example, if you ride a bus, subway or train, you can probably read or study as you travel. Some students have hung bulletin boards on bathroom walls or kitchen appliances to review formulas, vocabulary, or notes. One student taped her index cards near the kitchen sink to review while doing dishes. And for times when you eat alone, you can also read or study.

Scheduling Your Time

The most important way to gain control over time is to set up a schedule. Arranging a master schedule of everything you do will help you see just how you spend your time. It will also help you see where you can be flexible about your use of time and where you have to adjust to fixed routines, such as an evening job or child care responsibilities.

You can develop schedules for different purposes and different stretches of time. You can create a quarter-term or semester schedule based on your school's academic calendar and the syllabi for each of your courses. You can make a monthly schedule using an ordinary calendar. And you can make weekly and daily schedules, blocking out chunks of time for your activities and responsibilities.

Using a Daily Planner

A daily planner simply lists hours of the day and days of the week, and leaves spaces to fill things in. Busy executives and professionals are never without their date books so they can immediately assess their other commitments when something comes up. Use a large-sized desk calendar with blocks for each hour, carry a pocket-sized version, or post sheets on the wall. You may need to experiment to find which works best for you.

Whatever you choose, the most important thing is to have it readily accessible. Whether you keep it in your pocket or purse, stick it on the refrigerator or wall of your dorm room, set it on your desk, or a combination of these locations, you need to always keep it handy to use for deciding what you are going to do, when. You are continually making decisions about how much time you are going to spend on study, recreation, friendships, work, volunteer activities, committee meetings, your favorite TV programs, eating and sleeping—all the things that are competing for those 24 hours of each day. This simple device helps you maintain the balance that best meets your priorities and preferences. Keeping it in front of you makes clear the realities of prior commitments and the trade off if you add something more.

Priorities and Planning

There are so many interesting and enjoyable things out there that most of us have trouble saying no. The most difficult part of time management is setting priorities, making hard-nosed, realistic decisions about how much time you are going to allocate to all these possibilities during what parts of the day or week. Your priorities will rest on three things: your basic obligations, responsibilities, and commitments; your values; and your interests or things you do for relaxation and enjoyment.

Most of us have responsibilities and commitments to meet while going to college. You may work full or part-time. You may have kids to get to or from school, meals only you can prepare, shopping only you can do. You may need to spend at least one weekend a month with parents. You may be committed to church or community activities. Your values lie behind many of these commitments, but they also influence your priorities for using discretionary time. Every choice, every act, every dollar you spend, is a value statement. Most adults returning to college have experienced value conflicts in choosing between studying, spending time with friends, partner, or children, and doing something for their own pleasure. Most residential students experience value conflicts in choosing among time with friends, getting heavily involved in extracurricular activities, and studying. Make time in your schedule for the things that are important to you, even if it means taking time away from something else.

Getting Started

If you are not already using a calendar or a planner, here is a basic strategy that works well for many people to get started and translate priorities into behavior:

1. List all the things you have to do and want to do.

2. Beside each item put the amounts of time you need or want to give to it.

3. Give each item a score from 1 to 5, with #1 standing for the things most important to you, or the things you just have to do, and #5 the least.

4. On a month-to-month calendar, work your way down the list. First block out the times required by certain recurring commitments, like classes, a job, athletics, helping kids with homework, commuting. Then put in the other activities at the times that seem to work best for you. Begin with the ones and end with the fives.

5. Now enter all the deadlines you have for future projects or performances: the dates when exams will be given or when papers are due, when one major task where you work needs to be completed, when you have to have the house ready for a party or for guests. Then put in the appropriate amounts of lead time so these important items don't get shortchanged because they've crept up on you.

A monthly time frame is useful because there are important things you want to do that don't happen every week: going to visit parents or having guests visit you; and special events like concerts, conferences, parties, children's performances, athletic events, and such. You need to keep this calendar on an ongoing basis, writing in future events or activities that are high priorities for you. Then you can anticipate them and change your weekly schedule accordingly. The present week and the week coming up will be the fullest and most detailed. Future weeks will probably have some windows of time here and there. It's a good idea to protect those blank spaces as long as possible to leave room for the unexpected things that come up.

Fitting it All In

If you are lucky, you may find all the time you need for your commitments and other things you want to do. Most of us are not so lucky. We have to either eliminate some activities or reduce the time given to them. So you will probably need to take the next step. Starting with your number five priorities, reduce or eliminate the time given to them until you have a schedule that, given the finite number of hours available, best fits your priorities. Note: You may be able to satisfy some fives by doing them only once or twice a month instead of every week.

There is another way to identify your priorities and develop your calendar for more intentional planning that may work better for you. This approach helps if you already keep a calendar. It goes like this:

◆ Create a detailed time log for the last week or two. The further back you can go accurately, the better. Include every hour of the day, or break it into half hours. Record as precisely as you can how all those hours were spent.

◆ List each activity and rank it from 1 to 5 according to its importance to you.

◆ Add the amount of time spent on each activity.

◆ Examine the fit between your priority rankings and the amount of time you are investing, and identify where there are big discrepancies.

◆ Modify your schedule for the next week or two to mini-mize the discrepancies and improve the fit between your considered priorities and your actual behavior.

Whichever approach you use, it is critical to treat this calendar as a living document. Which it is: It's your life. These are your priorities, whether they are expressed simply through the way you behave or expressed more consciously through explicit attention. These priorities will undoubtedly change with experi-ence, and as new interests, friendships, activities, obligations arise. In fact, one of the most useful things you can do is to examine your priorities and alter your schedule from time to time, perhaps at midterm, the end of the semester, or when some serious or meaningful change presents itself.

In the work world, urgent items can often override important ones. You get very busy putting out fires or reacting to pressing short-term, perhaps trivial, needs. Vital areas that have long-term significance, but which are not so compelling, are neglected until they become crises. The workaholic who is driven by the immediate needs of the job, who neglects a spouse and children and wakes up divorced or alienated, is a classic case. Research projects, term papers, building relationships with faculty members or fellow students, can be similarly neglected if time is not specifically reserved for them.

Defeat Procrastination

Finally, all the schedules in the world won't help you if you never use them, so be aware of the ways in which you procrastinate before making a schedule. Everyone procrastinates, but listening to the messages you give yourself can help to keep procrastination to a minimum. You may be telling yourself that you will not do a good job; you may not be sure exactly what to do; you may be a perfectionist and have set up impossibly high standards for yourself. Maybe you feel angry about doing the work at all. Whatever the excuse, identify what you think and feel about the task. It may not make it easier, but you may be able to minimize your procrastination. Here are some techniques to help you beat procrastination:

◆ Ask for help. If you realize that you're not sure exactly how to complete an assignment or study for a test, talk to the professor, another student, or a tutor about the task.

◆ Use the salami technique. Cut up large tasks into smaller segments, and list them on a piece of paper. Complete one of the tiny segments, and enjoy the feeling of accomplishment.

◆ Try the thirty-minute plan. Work on the task in thirty-minute segments.

◆ Do the hardest part first.

◆ Talk to yourself. Say aloud what you are going to do and

when. Tell yourself you are capable of doing an adequate
job.

◆ Lower your standards. Sometimes average is fine. You don't
   need to always be brilliant. Just get the job done.

The time management skills you develop now will benefit you for
the rest of your life. Try different ways of organizing your time,
find the one that works best for you, and stick with it. You will be
amazed how much more you accomplish in the same 24 hour
day.

*This chapter was adapted from the following Allyn & Bacon
books:*

Montgomery, Rhonda J., Patricia G. Moody, and Robert M.
Sherfield. Cornerstone: Building on Your Best. 1997.

DiYanni, Robert. How to Succeed in College. 1997.

Chickering, Arthur W., Nancy K. Schlossberg. Getting the Most
Out of College. 1995.

Laskey, Marcia L., Paula W. Gibson. College Study Strategies:
Thinking and Learning. 1997.

2

Effective Notetaking

"The mind is like the stomach. It is not how much you put into it that counts, but how much it digests." **—A.J. Nock**

It is reasonable to expect that you will spend twelve or more hours per week attending lectures. Needless to say, you will be getting a lot of auditory information. Because you will forget about 60% of a lecture within an hour after class, notes will become a valuable record to use for review and studying for tests.

Developing Notetaking Skills

The first rule for good notetaking is to be prepared. One kind of preparation involves the studying you do before class—reading assigned chapters or pages, doing problems and exercises, bringing in drafts of written work as required. Another kind of preparation involves bringing the necessary tools to class—the right books and notebooks, pens, pencils, portable computer, tape recorder—whatever you need to take good notes.

Being prepared in these ways, though necessary, is not sufficient. You also need to attend to additional matters. Some, like finding a good place to sit, are simple; others, like listening attentively, are more complex and may require effort, practice, or a change in habit.

Finding a Place to Sit

Find a place in the classroom where you are comfortable and from which you can see and hear the instructor. The closer to the front you are, the better you will be able to see and hear and the fewer distractions you will receive from other students. Choosing a seat that is in a well-lit area and away from a humming air conditioner or a blowing heater may require you to come a few minutes early. But being in a good spot enables you to concentrate better on classwork and makes notetaking easier.

Listening

We often take listening for granted. Learning how to listen is critical for academic success. You can improve your listening skills by following these guidelines.

Listening Guidelines

1. Be a willing rather than a reluctant listener. Expect to hear something interesting. Listen for the unexpected detail, the unusual example.

2. Be a focused rather than a distracted listener. Concentrate on what is being said. Refocus when your mind wanders.

3. Be an engaged listener rather than an unengaged listener. Find ways to connect what is said with what you know. Identify key points and supporting details. Don't stop listening out of boredom or disagreement.

4. Be an active rather than a passive listener. Try to anticipate where the lecture may be going at different points.

5. Ask questions about anything unclear, no matter how simple you think your question may be. Other students may have the same questions.

6. Participate as much as you can. Add your own comments to those of other students.

Participating in Class

Many classes require participation. The degree of participation from one course to another may vary considerably—from classes in which an occasional student asks a rare question to classes in which group discussion is the norm. Instructors differ, sometimes radically, in how they initiate or discourage class discussion. But whether or not your classes require participation, you should try to participate as fully as possible.

By becoming actively involved in class, you keep focused, and you take better notes on the important aspects of the discussion. You also have a greater chance of remembering material enlivened by class discussion, especially if you participated actively.

Notetaking Techniques

Taking notes in lecture courses involves more than trying to write down as much as you can while the instructor speaks. You need to be selective, to write down the essential concepts and ideas along with as much supporting information as enables you to understand the day's lesson.

For courses in which instructors provide well-organized lectures, simply following their lead in recording the major points made will generally result in reasonable, well-organized notes, especially if you can identify headings for your notes. In courses where instructors do not provide a clear sense or organization, you will have to work harder to take well-organized notes. The important thing is for you to sort the information and concepts in a logical way that makes sense to you.

Some Suggestions for Notetaking

Here are a few things you can do to make effective use of your notes.

1. Sit near the lecturer. Sitting as close as possible makes it easier for you to hear the lecture, read the material on the chalkboard or overhead, and concentrate on what's being

said.

2. Organize both your class and your reading notes. At the very least, use separate notebooks, or sections of a loose leaf binder, for different courses.

3. Label and date your notes. The date will tell you at what point in a course you covered specific material. The label will help you quickly locate topics you may wish to review.

4. Use your own shorthand. Devising your own shorthand makes the recording process faster and less tedious. Use an abbreviated form of any words that are used often Here are some examples:
   and = & or +
   with = w/
   example = i.e. or ex.
   different = diff
   organization = org

5. Make your handwriting as legible as possible. Leaving wide margins and blank lines between paragraphs and lists makes the notes easier to read or add to later.

6. Listen to the lecturer's clues. Some phrases that indicate main ideas are ones such as "Three causes are..."; "An important point is..."; "Six characteristics are..." When you hear phrases such as these, be sure to include the information in your notes.

7. Separate your comments and observations from the ideas of your instructor and from the authors of the texts you read. If you wish to use your notes in a paper or other assignment, you will have an easier time identifying your own ideas.

8. Edit and revise your notes. Go through your notes after class to make handwriting legible, to fill in missing words, and to add details. Later, you may wish to add additional related notes in a different ink color. Review your notes periodically to help retain the information.

Alternatives to Independent Notetaking

Some students find it difficult to take notes while listening to lectures. Thus, much information is lost. When this situation occurs, you should consider alternatives such as the following:

1. Ask a fellow student to take notes for you. This can be done by using a carbon or by making photocopies of the original notes.

2. Ask the professor to arrange for a student in the class to volunteer to be class notetaker. The notes are placed in a central location immediately after class so the notes can be picked up.

3. Ask the appropriate staff person within the university to make arrangements for a notetaker. Sometimes the university will provide professional student notetakers on a paid or volunteer basis.

4. Audiotape the lectures (be sure to get the instructor's permission first). Remember, however, that it takes time to play back lectures on a tape recorder, so you are committing to what may amount to twice the class time. Use the pause button when taping so you only tape essential information. Be sure to take as many written notes as you can even when you are taping so that you remain an active listener during lecture. Review the tape as soon as possible after lecture to make necessary additions to your notes.

Taking Notes From Your Text

Another type of note taking is done when you read your text. You should take notes from your text because it will aid your concentration and memory, just as it does when you take notes from a lecture. Notes from textbooks can consist of highlighting, marginal annotations, and summary systems. Just as you forget lecture material if not written in notes, you do not remember reading material as readily if you do not mark your texts. These textbook notes can then be used when studying for a test.

When you highlight, annotate, or summarize, you select the main ideas and important terms more efficiently. You will be more likely to understand and remember what you have read if you are actively involved with the reading material.

Checklist for Notetaking

Before lecture

1. Read the related textbook material.
2. Look at course outlines and objectives.
3. Review previous notes.
4. Anticipate lecture content.
5. Discuss ideas with classmates.

During lecture

1. Attend the lecture.
2. Sit where you can see and hear.
3. Have your mind set to listen.
4. Listen actively for main ideas.
   a. Use title for headings.
   b. Note speaker's pattern of ideas.
   c. Be alert to speaker's voice and gestures.
   d. Copy down material written on the chalk board or overheads.
5. Record notes in an organized form.
   a. Write legibly.
   b. Leave a margin on the left for additional notes.
   c. Leave space between ideas.
   d. Write in sentence form.

After lecture

1. Revise and review lecture notes immediately after class.
2. Reflect on notes; relate them to the textbook.
3. Review notes frequently to retain information.

This chapter was adapted from the following Allyn & Bacon books:

Hamachek, Alice L. <u>Coping With College</u>. 1995.

Laskey, Marcia L., Paula W. Gibson. <u>College Study Strategies: Thinking and Learning</u>. 1997.

DiYanni, Robert. <u>How to Succeed in College</u>. 1997.

3

Improving Study Skills and Memory

"There is no easy method of learning difficult things. The method is to close the door, give out that you are not at home, and work."
—Joseph de Maistre

As you already know, study skills are intimately related to notetaking skills. Some additional aspects of studying include the following topics:

1. Finding an appropriate place to study
2. Mapping out a schedule of study time
3. Setting goals for study sessions
4. Learning to focus and concentrate
5. Increasing your understanding of what you study
6. Remembering what you study

Finding a Suitable Study Environment

Some students swear that they study best in bed—prone or propped up by pillows. For most, however, this place and position is an invitation to study disaster. Your body "knows" when it is in bed, and prepares itself for sleeping rather than studying. Better than your bed is a desk or table with ample room for you to spread out your books, papers, notes and other materials. You might set yourself up at a library desk or table, in a room in your home or in a campus residence hall—as long as the place allows you to work without distractions.

You should study in a place free of distractions—no radio blaring, no MTV, no friends stopping by to chat, no children seeking attention. And it should also be well enough lit for you to read comfortably.

Mapping Out a Schedule of Study Time

As important as an appropriate place to study is adequate time. Ideally, you should try to study at times when you are most alert and work your best. Whatever your optimum study time is, try to ensure that you schedule your study hours for that time. Most important is that you study your most difficult and demanding subjects during your optimum study times. You should also study those subjects first, while your mind is at its best.

But reality may interfere with your study schedule. When circumstances prevent you from studying during your optimum time, you need to have other regularly scheduled study. Allocating sufficient time to prepare for classes, review your notes, complete reading and writing assignments, and study for quizzes, tests, and exams is crucial for academic success.

Setting Goals for Studying

Whether you are settling in for a long study session for a major exam or just squeezing in a short period to review for a quiz, you should have a specific goal for your study session. Before you get down to work, determine what you want to accomplish and how long you plan on studying to reach your goal.

For long study sessions, set small goals with shorter time periods within your overall session and overall goal. If, for example, you need to review three chapters for a midterm during a single study session, you should break up your study period into three blocks of time and set a specific goal for each. When you start or finish your second study session on this material, you should also review the main points of the first session. For the third session, do a quick review of the main points you studied in the first two sessions. Three 1-hour sessions are preferable to one marathon 3-hour session. The shorter sessions give you a chance to review and reinforce what you learn. You will also be less apt to tire and can thus retain more of what you learn.

Taking Breaks

To make efficient use of your time, it is necessary to take breaks from concentrated periods of study. There are limits to how long we can concentrate, just as there are limits to how many things we can hold at once in our short-term memory. In a 2-hour study session, for example, you may need a break after 50 or 55 minutes, allowing you to relax and then return to concentrate better than you would have without taking the break. To avoid stretching breaks beyond 5, or perhaps 10 minutes, you can use a kitchen timer or radio alarm.

Learning to Concentrate

Having a study schedule and setting goals to achieve them will not be of much use unless you can concentrate and focus your intellectual energy on your study tasks. To concentrate means to zero in on what you wish to read, learn, and think about. To do that, you need to find ways to shut out distractions, both external and internal.

Essential for concentration is a quiet environment and one in which you have everything you need to do your work. Beyond external quiet, you may need to make an effort to shut out distracting thoughts and create internal quiet. Try to become absorbed in the details of your work and try to avoid giving in to distracting thoughts of what you'll be doing later. When you catch yourself daydreaming or thinking about something other than the task, stop yourself and direct your mind back to your work.

It is also essential to have adequate rest and enough to eat. Eating too much before studying, however, can make you both physically and intellectually sluggish. You will probably do better with a small edge on your appetite.

Improving Understanding

The following strategies for studying can enhance your understanding of course materials.

1. Translate into your own words what you recorded from your instructor in class or what you copied from a textbook. When you are able to translate a concept into your own words by paraphrasing or summarizing it, you demonstrate to yourself that you really do understand it.

2. Sometimes it is helpful to come at a concept from a different perspective. Convert words you read or heard into diagrams or pictures that illustrate the idea or process described. Visualizing a process by representing it in a diagram and labeling its parts or stages not only helps you "see" it better, but also helps you remember the process.

3. Associate what you are learning with what you already know. Link the new and unfamiliar with old and familiar knowledge. All learning, essentially, involves connecting what you don't know with what you do. In fact, if you cannot relate new information and new ideas to what you already know, you won't really learn them or remember them—that is, you won't be able to use new ideas and information until you can relate them to what you have already learned.

4. Preview what you are studying when you start (a chapter of a textbook, for example). Previewing a text involves looking it over quickly before diving in deeply and reading and studying it carefully. Previewing gives you a chance to survey the text overall. You can see where it starts, where it ends, and what ground it covers in between. You can also gain an overview of how one part of the overall text for study relates to other parts.

5. Review quickly when you finish studying. A brief review of what you covered during an entire study session helps you do two things—see relationships among parts of the material, and solidify them and reinforce what you learned as you focused on the individual parts. Review is an essential part of the study process, and should be a regular part of your study habit.

Memorizing

You may find it necessary to memorize facts and figures, formulas and sequences of events. Sometimes a major test is given with the assumption that you can remember many of the things you learned for earlier quizzes. If so, you'll need to review them and put them back in memory.

Useful rules exist for memorizing anything, whether you are learning it for the first time or relearning it.

1. *Focus.* Concentrate on what you are memorizing. If it's a piece of music, listen with your full attention. If it's a sequence of biochemical processes, look at the whole sequence and then break it into its parts. Focus on those small parts. Then put them back together. Analyze, or break the work down into small pieces. It's easier to memorize small elements than large ones.

2. *Associate.* Try to connect what you are memorizing with something else. You may recall learning the names of the lines of the musical staff (E-G-B-D-F) by associating those lines with the first letter of each word in this sentence: Every Good Boy Does Fine. You may have learned other things by means of rhyme.

3. *Repeat to Reinforce.* Repetition is another useful technique for memorizing things. Ideally, you should memorize what you need to know early so you have time to reinforce it, thus impressing it more firmly in your mind when you review.

Reviewing to Remember

One of the best ways to remember what you learn in your study sessions is to review. You can use review three ways:

1. Review immediately after studying.

2. Repeat the review periodically—at the beginning of each study session.

3. Review cumulatively; that is, review the material from all previous study sessions at the beginning or end of each successive study session.

Other Techniques for Aiding Memory

To remember something, you must want to remember it. Your intention is important. If you don't care about remembering a name, a date, a process, or a theory, you won't remember it. Think of how often you forget things you don't care about and remember what's important to you.

In deciding whether to intend to remember material for your courses, you must consider whether the material is important. Is it important enough to be on a test? Is it important enough in its own right—is it of immediate interest to you?

You will have more success in remembering course materials when you organize and categorize what you learn. In learning to conjugate French verbs, study them in clusters or groups—*Er* and *Ir* verbs, for example. In learning about the history of philosophy, group philosophers according to whether they are Aristotelians, who begin with concrete sense experience, or Platonists, who begin with abstract ideas. You can group composers by their musical styles—Classical and Romantic, for example, or by their historical periods—medieval, Renaissance, Baroque, and so on.

Still other strategies to help you solidify and remember what you study include using more than one of your senses. Typically, you study silently, reading words on a page, perhaps hearing them soundlessly in your mind. You can try saying aloud what you want to remember. You can tape important information and play it back so you hear it. You can also walk around from time to time when you study, perhaps reciting aloud what you are trying to learn. The rhythm of your walking and the echo of your voice can lodge more deeply what you might study in silence.

Cramming

Cramming is an attempt to commit large amounts of information to memory in marathon study sessions. Cramming can overload your memory circuits so that you confuse things wildly. This confusion is especially likely if you are studying an unfamiliar subject with strange terminology, and you've let it go until a marathon cramming session. Such cramming is dangerous. At best, you will remember some things because they'll be fresh in your mind. At worst, you'll confuse what you've memorized, and you'll embarrass yourself. At most, even if you're reasonably successful and manage to avoid the pitfalls of cramming, how much will you actually remember? You may remember some of what you study, but only for a short time. If you are really interested in learning, if you're concerned about real academic success, and if you want to develop your intellectual powers, you'll not cheat yourself by making cramming your primary method of study. In an emergency, as a last resort, for the material you've already studied, it's all right. Otherwise, it's not.

This chapter was adapted from the following Allyn & Bacon book:

DiYanni, Robert. How to Succeed in College. 1997.

Taking Tests

"Three-fourths of the mistakes a man makes are made because he does not really know the things he thinks he knows."
—James Bryce

Since your grades and academic profile throughout your academic career are tied to being tested, it makes sense to learn how to perform well on examinations. Doing well on tests depends on being well prepared for them.

This is not news to you. After all, no one who goes through a dozen years of school tests and takes standardized tests for college admission is unfamiliar with the importance of tests. What may be new, however, is the notion that you can use specific techniques and strategies to improve your performance. Your improved performance will reflect enhanced understanding and greater learning. In short, your higher test scores will reflect your stronger grasp of the subjects you are being tested on.

Adequate Preparation

Students who don't prepare well for tests often experience panicky feelings simply because they do not know the subject thoroughly. They have crammed right before the test or have not allowed enough time in their schedules to prepare for the test adequately. Since fear feeds on itself, once students experience several episodes of test anxiety, they are more likely to associate test taking with anxiety whether they are well prepared or not.

Therefore, being well prepared for the test is a must for reducing test anxiety.

As part of preparing for tests, a student needs to be in good physical condition by getting plenty of sleep and eating regularly. Plan your study schedule realistically, so you will have time to eat regular meals, get enough sleep, and exercise regularly. Setting up a schedule will help you feel in control of yourself and the situation. It will also help you feel well physically.

Preparation for a test should begin at least a week to three days before the test. In fact, continuous review and good study strategies are the best methods for preparing for taking tests. Finally, you need to consider how to study. Following are guidelines to use when trying to determine the what, where, when, and how of studying for a test.

What
1. All major sources of information
2. Textbook chapters
3. Lecture notes
4. Previous exams and quizzes
5. Teacher handouts
6. Course outline
7. Any outside of class assignments

Where
1. A place where there can be no interruptions
2. The library
3. Your usual study place

When
1. Several hours for study each day of the week
2. Several review sessions at least a week in advance of test
3. The day before the exam—once through entire review

How
1. Organize the review
2. Begin by going through all your material
3. Sort out those areas in which you need work and concentrate on them
4. Select a procedure based on the type of exam. For objectives tests, you need only to recognize information. For essay tests, you need to recall information.
5. Predict questions that will be asked on the test.

6. Develop a study system.

Test Anxiety

No one is immune to performance anxiety. Actors, athletes, public speakers, all have reactions ranging from mild butterflies to cold sweats. It's normal and healthy to feel nervous or uptight before an exam. The tension helps you to be alert, sharpens your reflexes, gets your juices running. It can also lead to panic, confusion, and mental blocks.

The best moderator of test anxiety, of course, is thorough, ongoing learning beforehand. But there are other things you can do to be ready:

◆ Get your normal amount of sleep.
◆ Do some aerobic exercise to burn off a bit of that extra energy.
◆ Play a game you enjoy, or do something else just for fun.
◆ Have some water and a bit of fruit before you go in.
◆ Do some deep breathing and relaxation exercises.
◆ Tense and relax muscle sets: feet, legs, arms, neck torso.
◆ If you are getting some strong physical reactions, visualize their location in your body and describe them to yourself.
◆ Do some creative visualization, seeing yourself at the beach, in the mountains, soaking in the tub.

When you get the exam, look it all over. Identify the questions you know well and those that will take more hard thinking. If you feel blocked on some questions, set them aside. Once you get into the other questions the block may disappear. If there are some questions that are totally beyond you, don't try to fake them. Simply say what little you know, or indicate you can't respond, and concentrate on doing your best on the rest.

Test Taking Strategies

You can develop skills and strategies for test taking. These skills are no substitute for thorough preparation, but they will help you perform in ways that accurately reflect your knowledge and competence rather than short-changing it.

Essay Exams

When you are answering an essay question, follow these basic steps:

◆ Make sure you understand the question. Most instructors are surprised how often students simply misread the question. When asked to critique an argument, or contrast different theories or concepts, or evaluate the evidence for an assertion, they will simply describe the ideas. When asked to list, they will explain. When asked to outline, they will narrate or summarize. If you misunderstand the question, there is no way to do well.

◆ Brainstorm. Write down key words or abbreviations for all the ideas that come to mind as potential responses. Brainstorming can be especially important if you feel a bit shaky about how much you know. Once you get into it, you will find other relevant information coming to mind.

◆ Plan your answer. Some people find it helpful to create a brief outline, or simply jot down key words or phrases that signal ideas you want to include. You don't necessarily have to get down everything you might want to say. Just try to get a good structure.

◆ Get clear about how much time you have for the question. Think through how much detail or how many illustrations you can include for each major point.

◆ Be brief and to the point. Your purpose is to reveal how much you know. If the teacher and exam permit, you may find it most effective to use telegraphic language and an outline rather than full sentences. You can cover more territory that way. If you like that approach, clarify whether it is okay before the exam.

◆ Leave lots of space as you write. If you are given an exam booklet, use just the right or left page and leave the other side blank. As you move through your answer, you often will remember content that should have been included earlier.

Leaving space between your key sections or on the opposite page makes room for these insertions. They will be easy for the teacher to read and recognize where they go.

◆ If time permits, reread your completed response. Often that rereading will identify things that need to be clarified, or additional points you want to make.

Multiple Choice and True-False Exams

Multiple choice and true-false exams, especially those composed by teachers who are not experts in test making, often contain internal clues that help you eliminate wrong answers and identify right ones. They will also contain questions you immediately know and others where you are uncertain. The most important thing is to go through and first answer every question you are sure of. Answer each question in your head before looking at the options. If you can do that, you are likely to choose the correct response.

Then you need to know whether you will be penalized for incorrect answers. To protect against guessing, test scoring sometimes deducts 20 or 15% of your wrong answers from your right ones. When that is the case, you have to be more calculating about guessing on the basis of clues other than your own sure knowledge. You need to eliminate alternatives so that your chances are one out of two instead of one out of four or five. But if there is no penalty, don't hesitate to make your best guesses. Here are some internal clues you may find helpful:

◆ Be alert for answers suggested by other questions. A concept, fact, or piece of information may be supplied or implied elsewhere in the test.

◆ Options that use absolute words like *always, never, all, none, only*, and the like are rarely correct.

◆ If the answer offers sentence completions, eliminate options that don't result in grammatically correct sentences.

◆ Eliminate options with incorrect details.

◆ If two options are similar, choose one: if two options contain similar quantities, choose one.

Matching Exams

Matching exams are a bit more difficult than simple multiple choice or true-false exams. They don't lend themselves to guessing unless you accurately eliminate most of the alternatives. Do all the match-ups you are sure of first. Cross out both parts if the exam format permits. Then you can clearly distinguish the remaining alternatives.

Avoiding Cheating

With the pressures to succeed in college, you may observe students cheating. You yourself may be tempted to cheat. In any and all cases, do not. If you're unprepared for a   surprise quiz, suffer the consequences and be better prepared next time. If you're tempted to copy answers from other students on big tests, or if you're inclined to buy a term paper rather than write your own, you need to consider why. And you need to consider the consequences of your actions, whether or not you get caught.

Besides being a form of theft, cheating undermines the integrity of academic institutions. To participate in the work of an academic community requires abiding by its rules and accepting its conventions. Cheating violates those conventions.

One type of cheating, plagiarism, involves appropriating the ideas of another and pretending they are yours. When you use someone else's ideas or words, whether you use them in a paper or speech, you must credit your source. Not to do so, claiming ownership of words or ideas you did not develop on your own, is dishonest. Colleges and universities take plagiarism very seriously; some, in fact, dismiss students for plagiarizing.

Be sure you understand the different forms plagiarism can take. And be sure you understand different instructors' definitions of the term. Consult a good college handbook, and talk about plagiarism with your advisor or with one of your instructors.

This chapter was adapted from the following Allyn & Bacon books:

DiYanni, Robert. How to Succeed in College. 1997.

Laskey, Marcia L., Paula W. Gibson. College Study Strategies: Thinking and Learning. 1997.

Chickering, Arthur W., Nancy K. Schlossberg. Getting the Most Out of College. 1995.

5

Coping With Stress

"The greater the obstacle the more glory in overcoming it." —Moliere

As you begin your college career, you will discover that learning certain strategies and understanding what college life is all about will ease your adjustment to higher education. It is to your advantage to assess your goals, attitudes, learning style, and academic strengths and weaknesses as you begin this new experience. In a sense, when you enter college, you leave your old life behind. You will probably view your old job, neighborhood, friends, and school in a new light as you become involved with college life, which has its own values, assumptions, customs, traditions, and activities.

Adapting to this new environment demands extra physical and mental energy as you learn new information and develop new skills. Adjusting to these changes can create stress. You can learn to cope with stress and ensure that college will be an enriching, productive experience.

Stress

Stress is emotional and physical tension, which accompanies any positive or negative change. Learning to deal with stress is an important beginning in adjusting to your new environment. You can't avoid stress entirely, but you can change your response to it. The best place to start is to recognize what you can control and what you can't. You can't control other people, and you can't control every event that happens; however, you can control how you respond to people and events.

In today's rapidly changing world, almost everyone experiences stress. Some amount of stress is positive because it helps you achieve what you need to by increasing the adrenaline that gives you the energy to attain your goals. However, too much stress prevents you from being effective because it creates tension, which makes you less able to deal with the situation at hand. Entering college and adapting to a new life-style are stressful. Meeting new acquaintances, living away from home, and entering new social situations can all be difficult. Academic demands, deadlines, and exams add even more stress. In fact, the first year for all students is a venture into the unknown that can be quite terrifying. Too much stress may cause you to feel tense, anxious, uncomfortable, or even depressed. You might have the feeling that you will never be able to cope with this new situation.

Causes for Stress

Determining the cause of your stress is the first step toward coping with it. Situations, such as lacking career goals or indecision about changing careers, can cause stress. Academic concerns about grades, exams, finishing papers on time, and being able to complete all the assigned reading create stress for college students. Difficult relationships with roommates, friends and family can also create stressful situations. Finally, financial worries about whether there will be enough money for next semester's tuition can contribute to stress.

Negative Coping Strategies

There are both negative and positive ways to cope with stress. Although negative strategies may offer temporary relief, they do not help in the long run. Negative coping strategies include using alcohol and drugs, which ease the feeling of stress by dulling your feelings and lessening your self-awareness. However, they produce only a temporary release from the actual stress. Moreover, if alcohol and drugs become a way of life, you will no longer be able to function effectively in school and your focus will be on escape, not learning.

Becoming antagonistic, acting aggressively, and blaming others for your problems are other negative coping strategies that shift responsibility away from you, but these tactics are self-defeating because they alienate other people and don't solve the problem at hand. For example, you may blame a teacher for a poor grade, but, in reality, you are the one responsible. Stress can only be temporarily reduced by using negative coping strategies, so it is important to find positive alternatives.

Positive Coping Strategies

There are many positive strategies for dealing with stress. Once you identify the cause of stress, whether it is an exam or a social relationship, then you can deal with it. If it is school related, perhaps prioritizing your time and organizing your tasks will help to alleviate some of the stress. Or you may need to seek extra academic support. If the stress is emotional, you may want to find someone to talk to, either a friend or a professional counselor.

Other strategies involve changing your responses to the stress by setting more realistic goals, reducing the number of your obligations, being more positive, and using positive self-reinforcement. For instance, tell yourself that you can handle the situation, and then develop a plan to deal with it. Good physical health, regular exercise, and healthful eating and sleeping routines also play a part in helping you cope with problems more effectively. If you find that you are unable to develop a plan for dealing with the problems causing you stress, seek the advice of a counselor on campus for support.

Personal Resources

Using your personal resources won't make you totally immune to stress, but doing so will provide a foundation for you and give you a sense of control over your life. Your personal resources include your self-esteem, your goals, and your behavior.

Self-Esteem

Your most important, enduring resource is you—your belief in yourself as a capable, unique, and worthwhile person. This basic belief, often referred to as self-esteem, is based on our judgment of ourselves, not on other people's assessment. Our self-esteem is partially determined by our past relationships with family, friends, and coworkers. If your experiences in these areas are largely negative, then your self-esteem may be lower than it should be.

Setting Goals

Your goals are an important expression of who you are, and setting clear goals can relieve stress by giving you a sense of control over your life. Why are you attending college? What do you want to gain from the experience? These questions can make students uneasy because they are often difficult to answer. Whatever the reason you have chosen to come to college, examining your motives can be a good point to begin learning more about yourself.

If your reasons came mostly from the outside pressure of your family and friends, then your motives are largely extrinsic. For example, your family may continue to offer rewards, such as praise or money, for college success and punishment, such as disapproval or lack of funds, for poor performance. Friends and spouses may offer approval for your success in college or criticism for failures. Extrinsic motives can only be effective if the pressure from outside continues. They do not provide long-lasting or sustained support for your achievement. More important than extrinsic motives are your own values and the personal satisfaction you get from achieving your goals.

Your own goals and the sense of satisfaction you get from achieving them are intrinsic motives. Some intrinsic motives might include preparing for a satisfying career, gaining more information about the world, developing social skills and meeting new people, or living independently from your family.

Attendance

Your behavior is another personal resource you control, and

attending classes regularly and punctually is an important factor for success in college. As Woody Allen said, "Ninety percent of success is showing up!" If you do not attend class on a regular basis, you will miss some vital information needed to understand a new concept or to do well on an exam. Notes from a classmate are not as effective as your own because your knowledge base and learning styles are different. Therefore, what you need to know may not be in your friend's notes.

Teacher-Student Relationships

Another important resource is teacher-student relationships. Instructors, professors, and teaching assistants are all resources for students. If possible, try to develop a relationship with your instructor by seeking assistance with course work when needed. Always be polite and respectful toward faculty, but do not hesitate to ask questions or challenge ideas presented in class. All teachers are required to establish office hours when they are available to meet with students. Office hours and other important information can be found in your course syllabus, so read it carefully.

Student Relationships

Relationships with your fellow students are another important resource because they can provide general emotional support as well as support for individual classes. Study groups can be formed, or you can pair with another student so that you will be able to share ideas and information. Your friendships with other students can also make classes more enjoyable and less stressful.

This chapter was adapted from the following Allyn & Bacon book:

Laskey, Marcia L., Paula W. Gibson. College Study Strategies: Thinking and Learning. 1997.

Getting Motivated

"You will become as small as your controlling desire; as great as your dominant aspiration."
—James Allen

The first thing you need to know about motivation is that it comes from within—no one else can give it to you. Someone may temporarily inspire you, but on a daily basis you must reach down inside and find the will to motivate yourself. Your college experience will make hundreds of unique, life-changing opportunities available to you, but no one will force you to take advantage of these opportunities.

Motivation refers to whatever seems to lead you to do what you do, and think what you think. Some motives are rooted in basic impulses and needs for things like food, security, sex, and love and respect from others. Other motives are based on interests, aspirations for the future, talents, or personal characteristics we want to express. People who succeed in meeting their needs and achieving their goals share several characteristics. They are clear about what's driving them, what they want to do, where they want to go. They have clear purposes. They set high standards for themselves, work hard, and take risks. They have self-confidence.

Clear Purposes

"When the going gets tough, the tough get going." But you don't do that without clear purposes. Clear purposes that can help drive your college education include: vocational plans and aspirations; personal interests; and issues concerning values, life-style, and family. Being clear about these areas releases energy and excitement about academic studies, extracurricular activities, friends, and working relationships that help you make progress.

We use the term "vocational plans" in the broad sense of a "calling." There is a huge difference between a "vocation" and a "job." You can think of your career as a succession of jobs, or you can think of various jobs as contributing to some larger work or contribution. How you think makes all the difference. The key problem is finding a meaningful vocation within the job structure of our society. Alienation from work typically occurs because we can't find that calling within the jobs available. Work that is a vocation is the way many of us add meaning to our lives.

Between one- and two-thirds of all students change career plans and aspirations during college. That's good. It often means they have become clearer about themselves and what is important about their own strengths and weaknesses. It means they are having experiences which raise useful questions, that they are open to those experiences and trying to profit from them.

Balancing vocational plans and aspirations with personal interests, and at the same time taking account of life-style and family issues, is a complex task. The trick is to be clear enough about your purposes so they give meaning and coherence to your existence; so your motives provide good drive for your time, energy and emotion.

Values

Having purposes consistent with your values helps orient your life toward things you feel are worthwhile and desirable. The values that underlie Bill's choice of wildlife conservation will differ in important ways from those underlying Mary's decision to be a lawyer. In large measure, your values are what makes you unique. They are shaped as you grow up with your particular parents, in your particular community and culture. To make life, career, and educational decisions that lead you in satisfying directions, you need to be clear about which values are most important for you.

Self-Confidence

Self-confidence plays a vital part in whatever you do. We've all seen people choke under pressure. A champion tennis player double-faults at a critical point, or goes from "being in the zone" to hitting everything out or into the net. A person asked a difficult question stumbles and rambles, looking down or away. Our minds go blank and we blow an easy exam question.

Strong motivation depends on your sense that you can do what you set out to do, influence others, or have an impact on events. It rests on past successes and on learning from failures. Cognitive skills and interpersonal competence are important to a successful career. But they won't add up to much without self-confidence, without a strong sense of your own competence. People who can take action to solve problems and cope with difficulties have successful careers and satisfying lives. People who experience the world as a series of insurmountable obstacles do not.

Reward Yourself

Everyone enjoys an achievement more if there is a reward at the end. Recognize a job well done with a trip to the mall or dinner at your favorite restaurant. Whether it's completing a two-hour study session, getting a good grade on a test, or finishing your last final, take the time to feel good about your accomplishment.

This chapter was adapted from the following Allyn & Bacon books:

Montgomery, Rhonda J., Patricia G. Moody, and Robert M. Sherfield. Cornerstone: Building on Your Best. 1997.

Chickering, Arthur W., Nancy K. Schlossberg. Getting the Most Out of College. 1995.

7

Thinking Critically

"Learning without thought is labor lost; thought without learning is perilous."
—Confucius

When entering college, you will encounter many new challenges, ideas, and experiences. In order to respond productively to these new situations, you need to use effective thinking strategies. You already use many of these strategies, but becoming aware of a set of attitudes and strategies sometimes referred to as critical thinking can help make your college experience more profitable. The word critical means using careful judgment or evaluation. Accordingly, a critical thinker evaluates by asking questions, analyzing, or trying to make sense of a problem or situation. The word thinking involves the formulation of ideas, which includes forming concepts, solving problems, and reasoning. Critical thinking is a complex concept that refers to a collection of cognitive activities that often work together. In a sense, it involves thinking about thinking. Learning to think critically can involve the following cognitive abilities:

◆ problem solving
◆ logical thinking
◆ perspective and perception
◆ analysis
◆ evaluation of ideas
◆ decision making

You cannot succeed as a student by memorizing and spitting back information. You must apply what you have learned, and this involves critical thinking. For example, what good is it for a nursing student to memorize information about drugs but not be able to understand and apply the information when working in a hospital setting? Memorization might help you to make the right decision, but thinking critically is more likely to ensure a better outcome. Once you have grasped the theoretical elements of the information presented or read, you need to be able to apply the information. Tests, exams, and discussions require applying the information that you have learned, and this is where critical thinking becomes paramount to success in college.

Critical Thinking as a Process

Critical thinking is also important in college because you will be asked to absorb and integrate an extensive variety of information which will assist you in seeing the whole picture. Although you may feel that many of the courses you are taking are not related to each other, there are, in fact, processes that are common to them all. Critical thinking is one of these processes.

Critical thinking not only plays a role in your professional aspirations but also affects your entire life. You need to learn to think critically when making decisions in all areas of your life. Good decisions are generally based on sound, logical thinking. An example of acting illogically is choosing to major in science when this is the most difficult area for you to understand. In contrast, logical thinkers will ask themselves the following questions when choosing a major: What am I good at? What are my interests? What career will satisfy me the most? What are my strengths and weaknesses? Critical thinking can help you to make better decisions, to learn more effectively, and to apply and analyze what you know.

Become an Active Participant

Not only do you as a critical thinker need to activate your cognitive skills, but you also need to be an active participant in the thinking process. Active participation means engaging in a dialog with yourself or others to decide what your basic thoughts are and to analyze how you came to these conclusions. Were your conclusions based on available facts and information, or were they based on what others told you? By thinking about and sorting out available information, you will be able to begin the process of problem solving, which is an important part of thinking critically.

Personal Decisions

Another area in which critical thinking is important is your social life. Critical thinkers think for themselves and are not easily swayed by peer pressure. You will be exposed to many different types of people with many different values. You will need to make decisions that may affect your whole life. Will you be pressured into drinking or taking drugs? Will you focus on your social life, or will you work on building your academic skills? Whether you are entering school as a returning adult or a traditional-age student coming from high school, the decisions you make are important ones and need to be thought out carefully. Critically thinking is vital to all parts of your life.

Passive Versus Active Thinking

There are two kinds of thinkers: passive thinkers and active thinkers. Passive thinkers do not exercise their mental powers but rather follow others and also base their decisions on their first emotional response. An active thinker, such as Mr. Spock in Star Trek, thinks logically and only comes to a conclusion based on objective reasoning. Which type of thinker are you? Look at the characteristics of the active and passive thinkers listed below. Can you identify the characteristics that best fit your thinking? Can you add to this list?

Passive Thinkers
◆ Not thinking for yourself
◆ Allowing events to control you
◆ Allowing others to do your thinking
◆ Not making decisions for yourself
◆ Believing everything you hear and read
◆ Avoiding decisions and goal setting

Active Thinkers
◆ Engaging in the practice of solving problems, achieving goals, and analyzing issues
◆ Getting involved

◆ Taking initiative
◆ Analyzing and evaluating what you hear and read
◆ Realistically making decisions and setting goals

People who think creatively generally approach a problem differently than someone who thinks logically. No one always thinks creatively, or always logically, but rather a combination of the two. Knowing which direction you tend to lean will help you find a better balance between the two. Here is a summary of the similarities and differences.

Comparing Creative and Logical Thinking

◆ *Creative thinking* puts things together, synthesizing them. *Logical thinking* analyzes things, takes them apart.

◆ *Creative thinking* generates new ideas. *Logical thinking* develops and evaluates ideas that have already been formulated.

◆ *Creative thinking* explores many alternatives; it is unconcerned with being right in every particular. *Logical thinking* focuses on finding a single answer and being right at each step of the way.

◆ *Creative thinking* is inclusive, admitting all ideas no matter how trivial or outrageous they may seem. *Logical thinking* is selective, screening out and eliminating unpromising possibilities.

◆ *Creative thinking* is random. Moving backward as well as forward, in circles as well as in straight lines, it permits jumps beyond the next step in a logical sequence. *Logical thinking*, on the other hand, is linear and sequential. It moves from point to point in a straight line, allowing for no skips or gaps.

◆ *Creative thinking* forestalls judgment, deliberately delaying critical evaluation. *Logical thinking* encourages making judgments, assessing whether an idea or piece of evidence is valid.

- *Creative thinking* is questioning, tentative, provisional. It adds the hypothetical, the what if, to logical thinking's how. *Logical thinking* is more assertive, confident, sure of itself.

- Creative and logical thinking both ask *why?* In *creative thinking*, the *why* stimulates further thought. In *logical thinking*, the *why* answers a question or proposes a solution.

- *Creative thinking* encourages humor and fluidity; it is unsystematic and flexible. *Logical thinking* prizes seriousness and rigor; it is systematic and methodical.

Despite their differences, creative and logical thinking complement each other. You need to think creatively to generate ideas and logically to evaluate them. Developing skill in using both types of thinking in everyday life, in school, and at work will increase your chances of success and will provide you with the pleasure of developing your intellectual abilities.

This chapter was adapted from the following Allyn & Bacon books:

Laskey, Marcia L., Paula W. Gibson. College Study Strategies: Thinking and Learning. 1997.

DiYanni, Robert. How to Succeed in College. 1997.

8

Reading Critically

"To-day a reader, to-morrow a leader."
—W. Fusselman

When we speak of reading critically, we emphasize the important role of evaluating or judging ideas, not just passively taking them in. How can you develop critical reading skills? First let's think about the characteristics of the critical reader and then develop those characteristics in ourselves.

Characteristics of the Critical Reader

A critical reader is:

◆ skeptical
(Just because it's in print doesn't mean it is right.)

◆ fact-oriented
(Give me the facts and convince me that they are the relevant ones.)

◆ analytic
(How has the work been organized? What strategies has the reader used?)

◆ open-minded
(Prepared to listen to different points of view; not restricted by personal biases.)

- ◆ questioning
  (What other conclusions could be supported by the evidence?)

- ◆ creative
  (What are some entirely different ways of looking at the problem or issue?)

- ◆ willing to take a stand
  (Is the argument convincing? What is my position on the issue?)

Reasons for Reading

Reading is essential for the kinds of learning college requires. Heavy reading is expected of college students, reading that will also challenge you with its level of difficulty. The better you can read—the better you can understand and analyze what you read—the better you will learn.

We read for different reasons: to escape, to pass the time, to acquire information, to understand, to think, to learn, to experience, to enjoy ourselves. Our purposes differ, and so, too, do the ways we read. Sometimes we read less to understand than simply to acquire information, to collect facts and figures. Sometimes we read to understand writers' ideas or to share their experience. We may read to think through an issue or problem, to weigh and consider, to evaluate the merits of an argument, to make judgments and to better understand why we make the judgments we do.

Reading for Information

One of the most common reasons for reading is to acquire information. In the simplest form of reading-for-information, your goal may be to gather facts. You may want to know how to operate your VCR or how much it costs to travel from Chicago to San Francisco. You may want to know what happened in the United States during the first week of July in 1863. Or you may simply read a book or magazine out of curiosity or interest. Along the way, you will almost certainly pick up information. More important than absorbing facts and figures, however, is the need to relate such information to the writer's idea or point. Thus even though your primary aim in reading may be to find things out, you may also discover yourself thinking about the information you glean. Most of your college reading requires not merely that you obtain facts but that you understand the writer's point and then relate that point to what you already know.

Reading and Interpretation

To interpret is to make sense of something. You do this regularly in your everyday life. You make sense of what people say to you. You interpret the various gestures and looks people give you. You cannot avoid interpreting, nor should you. It is basic to everyday living, and it is essential for academic success.

Making Inferences

An inference is a statement we make about what we don't know based on what we do know. To infer is to think, to make a mental leap from information or details to an idea about that information or those details. Your inferences will lead you to an understanding about what you are reading.

Reading and Evaluation

In reading to evaluate, you may find yourself resisting the claims of the text. You may decide, for example, that a text's ideas are unconvincing or that you don't endorse its values. In reading to evaluate, your goal is different from understanding. Although you must understand a writer's point to make a fair and reasoned judgment about it, your goal in evaluative reading is to make a judgment, to consider the merits of the text.

The following questions can help you read evaluatively:

1. Have you heard this idea before? Where and in what con text?
2. Is the idea convincing? Why or why not?

3. Is the idea appealing? Do you like it? Why or why not?
4. Does this idea lead you anywhere? To another idea, perhaps? To additional kinds of support for it?
5. Does your own experience confirm the idea or cause you to question it?

In raising such questions and in tentatively answering them, you should give the writer's idea a fair chance. Try to consider the idea thoughtfully and carefully rather than simply rejecting it outright. Be aware also that your assessment of any idea can change.

Reading and Imagination

To read is to imagine. When we read, we imagine a voice in our heads, perhaps a person or persona—a figure or character behind the voice. That's the first way in which our minds activate our imagination in reading. Reading stimulates our imagination, calling it into active life.

Reading as Conversation

One way to experience what reading involves is to approach it as an interaction with the author. Imagine yourself in dialogue not simply with a text but with a person, with a writer whose voice you hear and whose mind you come to know. Imagining the writer behind the text and envisioning how the writer might respond to your queries and reactions to the text provides an additional way into a work. It can lead you to discover different things than you might not see with other approaches.

This chapter was adapted from the following Allyn & Bacon books:

Seyler, Dorothy U. Steps to College Reading. 1998.

DiYanni, Robert. How to Succeed in College. 1997.

9

Using The College Library

"Every man has a right to his opinion, but no man has a right to be wrong in his facts."
—Bernard M. Baruch

The library at your college or university is its single most valuable academic resource. During your first few days or weeks on campus, you should become familiar with your library's layout so you know how to find the books and articles you'll need to do research for your courses.

One way to get to know your library is through its staff. Ask them for their help in gaining familiarity with the library's resources. Another way to gain access to a large university library is to speak with older, more experienced students who have used the library's resources.

Library Book Classification Systems

Your college library catalogs books by classifying them into categories. Each category or type of book is given a particular series of numbers, letters, or both. The Dewey Decimal System uses numbers; the Library of Congress Classification uses a combination of numbers and letters, with letters taking precedence. Each letter in the Library of Congress system indicates a general subject area: *B* indicates works of philosophy, *C* and *D* historical works, *P* literature, and so on. In the Dewey Decimal System each group of numbers performs the same function:

100-199 indicates works of philosophy; 200-299 covers religion; 800-899 is literature, for example. College libraries use the Library of Congress classification. Here is a sample listing:

BF 469 H3 *[The book's call number]*
Hall, Edward T. 1914 *[The author and his year of birth]*
The hidden dimension *[The book's title]*
Garden City, N.Y., Doubleday, 1966 *[Publication information: city, state, publisher, and year of publication]*
xii, 201 p. *[There are 12 prefatory pages and 201 regular pages.]*
illus. Bibliography *[It contains illustrations and a bibliography.]*

Finding Books

To find books in your college library, you need to know two things. First, you have to find out how to access the listing of books. Second, you need to locate the books themselves.

Your books will be listed in a computerized catalogue accessed through on-line database computerized technology. You can access books by *title*, by *author*, and by *subject*. Although most computerized data catalogs include instructions for self-tutoring, you can and should find someone to show you how to operate the system. Computerized databases will speed your search for books, are easy to use, and provide enormous amounts of information.

Finding Periodical Articles

You can locate articles in popular magazines and scholarly journals any numbers of ways. First, you can find current issues of periodicals displayed in a special section, where you can use them in the library. If you need issues of magazines that are more than a few months old, you will probably need to access those periodicals either by means of the computerized database or by using one of the periodical indexes.

Besides printed indexes such as the *Reader's Guide to Periodical Literature* and the *Business Periodicals Index*, your library will almost certainly own microform indexes that index many of the same periodicals and the articles they contain. Microforms are rolls of film (microfilm) or sheets (microfiche) that are read on special machines.

Using Your Library's Special Resources

Your college library will probably have other resources besides books and periodicals. These may include:

Art collections—drawings, paintings, photographs, and slides

Audio collections—music CDs and tapes, audiocassettes of speeches, documentaries, and readings of literary works

Government documents—pamphlets, newsletters, reports, brochures, and summaries of hearings

Special collections—original manuscripts, rare books, and memorabilia

Video collections

CD-ROM database— on-line databases

Internet—access to the Internet and World Wide Web

Research Papers

The library is an essential part of doing research for papers or reports. Writing a research paper involves locating sources, evaluating those sources, reading to gain information, taking notes, and documenting your sources. The library can help you discover what is already known about a subject, what issues need further study, and what sources exist for you to utilize.

Larger libraries will have more resources for you to access, so it is best to start your search there. Academic libraries are especially good sources for scarce or highly specialized materials. Some colleges also have separate libraries for specific disciplines, such as law, medicine, or business, in which you may find resources that are not available in other libraries. If you want to use a library at a school you don't attend, you may be restricted to using the materials in the library rather than checking them out and taking them with you.

The Internet will allow you to access many university libraries' catalogs. For example, *Gopher* (yaleinfo.yale.edu) will provide you with a list of current library catalogs available on the Internet. Your school's reference librarian will be able to point out other online resources.

This chapter was adapted from the following Allyn & Bacon book:

DiYanni, Robert. How to Succeed in College. 1997.

10

Taking Advantage of Campus Resources

"To admit ignorance is to exhibit wisdom."
—Ashley Montagu

Using campus resources can make the transition to college life easier for both recent high school graduates and adults returning to the academic environment. First, identify people, offices, and departments that offer support. Then determine their various locations, hours, and services offered.

The Library and Computers

Two indispensable resources are the library and computer lab. Both have become so important in education that they are promoted as a selling feature at many institutes of higher education and are often the first stop for prospective students in a show-and-tell tour of a school. Some large schools have wired laboratories, libraries, and dorms with a network that permits students and faculty to communicate via the computer with each other, with the school, with other libraries, and with millions of other students, faculty, experts, and laypersons via the Internet and the World Wide Web at any time of the day or night. Check your school to see what is available so that you can utilize the computer for writing papers, practicing skills, and for general use. If you are not computer literate, consider taking a basic computer course to familiarize yourself with a computer. Computers are no longer an elective option but are a necessary tool in helping with your college career.

Learning and Writing Centers

Learning centers offer academic support, peer tutoring, testing, and counseling. They have become an important part of most colleges today and offer help to many students in many different ways. If you begin to feel overwhelmed or are dissatisfied with test scores, or need help with understanding math, try using the services of a learning center.

Writing centers may be staffed by full-time faculty or staff, or by part-time faculty and student peer tutors. One of the most pervasive misconceptions students have about writing centers is to see them merely as places for remediation. Consider the writing center instead as a place where writing is taken seriously, a place to obtain reactions to what you've written, suggestions for what you are working on but have not yet written, and ideas for revision. You will find books and articles, flyers and brochures containing useful ideas and helpful tips. See the writing center as an opportunity for academic growth, not as an emergency unit to visit only when you receive a negative grade on one of your papers.

Advising Center

Speaking to an advisor or seeking out a counselor at an advising center is important in choosing courses, planning your schedule, and choosing your major. Advisors are aware of the various options and opportunities that courses and majors offer. In many schools it is mandatory to meet with an advisor before scheduling classes, so be sure to use this service to your advantage.

Counseling and Health Centers

The counseling office may be located in the health center or nursing office, depending on the size of the school. When stress becomes too much to handle or you are having personal difficulties, the counseling center can offer support by helping you to talk about and work out your problems. Health problems are often related to stress, so using the health facilities is also important. Another reason to use the health center is to discuss any physical disabilities . The health office or nurse should be notified of your disability so assistance can be provided when and if it is necessary.

Career Planning

The career planning and placement services are one of your most important resources. These services typically include a wide array of occupational interest inventories, value-clarification exercises, goal definition and planning exercises, and other helpful devices. They also have up-to-date information about job trends, as well as local, regional, and national employment opportunities. They usually have job fairs and a stream of on-campus visits by employers. In addition, there are experienced counselors who can help you think things through.

Faculty

Faculty members whose background or expertise seem relevant to your interests are key resources. Seek them out. Ask them questions, not only about potential opportunities and areas of study, but also about other people you might talk with or resources you might tap. Often one of these faculty members will be your advisor. Try not to be put off by feeling that you should not bother "busy professors" about your issues. They are paid to be available to students. So think through the kinds of questions you have, the kinds of information you need, and then get on their calendar for an hour or so. If you are clearly motivated and reasonably well organized in advance, most faculty members will invest time and energy trying to be helpful.

Don't feel you need to wait until your junior or senior year. The best time to become acquainted with career planning services and to establish working relationships with faculty members is during your freshman and sophomore years. That's when you need to get perspective on how you can best use your college experiences in the services of purposes you value.

Other Services

Other areas of support may be the financial aid office, Registrar, dean of students, student government, and various clubs and activities. Be sure to read the college catalog and student handbook for a full picture of the unique resources available on your campus. Here are some organizations and activities you may be interested in or have need of:

Special Student Services

◆ Services for physically impaired students try to ensure that students who have physical limitations can participate in the same types of academic, social, and cultural experiences that are available to non-impaired students. These services may help students who are mobility impaired, hearing impaired, visually impaired, or emotionally impaired.

◆ Services for nontraditional students may include mature students who often have special needs that can be met only by administrators, professors, and peers who understand their circumstances. These services may provide assistance with housing, day care, or tutoring.

◆ Services for minority students include organizations such as the Asian Association and the African American Society, providing support, encouragement, opportunities, and cultural events tailored to the needs of specific minorities on campus.

◆ Many colleges enroll large numbers of students from abroad. Services for international students provide support and social and cultural activities for these students.

Greek and Honor Societies

Many colleges in the United States house some form of Greek society (fraternities and sororities) on campus. Greek societies provide a wide range of services to the college and community; they provide opportunities for leadership and developing inter-personal skills and allow men and women to grow and experience different situations in a supportive atmosphere. In the past, the system has been under fire for hazing, drinking, and drug abuse. These organizations have worked hard to dispel this negative image. Most fraternities and sororities have now required study time; honor local, state, and national drinking and hazing policies; and have community service programs. During rush, fraternities and sororities openly recruit new members through parties, socials, open houses, and invitations to meetings.

Honor societies may exist on your campus, such as Phi Beta Kappa (honors for four-year colleges), and Beta Alpha Psi (honors for Accounting students). To qualify for admission to an honor society, you must have completed at least one year of college. Many honors programs require your nomination by a faculty member or department chair. You may be required to maintain a certain grade point average. If you are inducted into an honor society, you will be able to list this major accomplishment on your resume and job applications.

Professional Organizations

The professional organizations found on most large campuses are student wings of larger organizations that serve professionals, such as pharmacists, educators, or social workers. If a professional organization is represented at your college, get involved. Your participation will generate contacts that can help you for the rest of your life. You will make friends and job contacts, be able to attend professional conferences, and become involved in activities that support your academic classes.

Military Organizations

You may already have been involved with a military organization in high school such as ROTC or junior ROTC. If you are hoping for a career in the armed forces or if you are a student who enjoys structure, regiment, and leadership, get involved in a military organization. Many prepare graduates for entrance into officer training schools.

Religious Organizations

Your campus may or may not offer organizations devoted to religion or a variety of worship services. Many schools offer nondenominational worship services. Religious organizations are intended to give students an outlet for the practice of specific religions.

Special-Interest Clubs

Special-interest organizations are popular on campuses across the nation. They serve the needs of students from every walk of life and with interests that vary from flower arranging to speaking German. Most academic and social clubs fall into this category.

Whatever your needs and interests are, chances are there will be an organization on campus which will enrich your college experience. Ask around, it's worth the effort.

This chapter was adapted from the following Allyn & Bacon books:

Laskey, Marcia L., Paula W. Gibson. College Study Strategies: Thinking and Learning. 1997.

DiYanni, Robert. How to Succeed in College. 1997.

Chickering, Arthur W., Nancy K. Schlossberg. Getting the Most Out of College. 1995.

Montgomery, Rhonda J., Patricia G. Moody, and Robert M. Sherfield. Cornerstone: Building on Your Best. 1997.

NOTES

NOTES

NOTES